Affiliate Marketing Breakout

Sandy   Smith

ISBN-13: 978-1505429626

ISBN-10: 1505429625

DEDICATION

Dedicated to all online entrepreneurs

Affiliate Marketing Breakout

Disclaimer

Reasonable care has been taken to ensure that the information presented in this book is accurate. However, the reader should understand that the information provided does not constitute legal, medical or professional advice of any kind. No Liability: this product is supplied "as is" and without warranties. All warranties, express or implied, are hereby disclaimed. Use of this product constitutes acceptance of the "No Liability" policy. If you do not agree with this policy, you are not permitted to use or distribute this product. Neither the author, the publisher nor the distributor of this material shall be liable for any losses or damages whatsoever (including, without limitation, consequential loss or damage) directly or indirectly arising from the use of this product. Use at your own risk.

Table Of Contents

Selling to Your List

Affiliate Marketing and the Social Web: A Brief Overview

Using Affiliate Data FeedsUsing Calls to Action

In Affiliate Marketing, You Get What You Put In

Affiliate Marketing Breakout

Introduction

The idea of companies paying salespeople commissions for selling their products has been around since time untold. When the Internet came along, it was only a matter of time before someone thought to devise a way to take the practice online. There is some debate about who pioneered the concept of affiliate marketing, but webmasters of adult websites were among the first to put it into practice in the mid-1990s.

Affiliate marketing has come a long way since then. It has expanded to every field in online sales. It has evolved into a practice with all sorts of nuances and techniques. It has made a lot of people a lot of money, and a whole lot more people a little money. According to Marketing Sherpa, in 2006, affiliates worldwide earned an estimated $6.5 billion dollars in commissions.

Those who are new to affiliate marketing often have high expectations. They hear the stories of affiliates who are making six figures a year just by promoting other people's products, and they get stars in their eyes. They eagerly sign up for lots and lots of programs, and they start counting the money in their minds. Unfortunately, many of them barely make enough to cover their website hosting, much less a profit.

Maybe you're one of those who became disillusioned after months of barely existent profits. Or maybe you've made some money, but you haven't achieved the success that you had hoped for. Either way, it's important to realize that you – yes, YOU – can make a steady income with affiliate marketing. You don't have to be some kind of guru to make it work. You just have to be determined and ready to do what it takes to succeed. In this report, you'll learn how to take your affiliate marketing business to the next level.

Affiliate Marketing Breakout

Why Do Some Affiliates Make So Much More Than Others?

Affiliate marketing isn't a job. It's a business opportunity. That means that there is unlimited moneymaking potential. But it also means that how much you make is proportional to how much work you put into it. That doesn't mean that you have to make it a full-time effort, but it does mean that you have to keep working at it. It's easy money, relatively speaking, but just signing up for a program and putting up a link or two doesn't guarantee instant income.

Whether you want to make a living doing nothing but affiliate marketing or are looking to generate a steady supplemental income, you must be willing to dedicate a certain amount of your time to it. And this is a big part of the reason why income varies so significantly between affiliates. Some believe that if they choose a program that performs well for others that the products will sell themselves, but it just doesn't work that way.

If you understand that being a successful affiliate requires commitment, you're ahead of the game. But it's still quite possible that you're not making as much as you'd like to, despite your best efforts. There are certain traits that so-called super affiliates possess that allow them greater earning potential. Some of these are:

They include affiliate marketing activities in their schedule. Telling yourself that you'll spend a certain number of hours a week working on it is nice, but if you don't set aside time specifically for that purpose, there's a good chance that you won't get around to it. Whether they decide to spend 2 or 20 hours a week on affiliate marketing, super affiliates pencil it in on their calendars and stick to it.

They're not afraid to spend some money. You can become an affiliate for free, but if you're serious about bringing in regular income, you'll probably need to invest a little cash into it. Super affiliates realize this, and they have no qualms about spending on site building, pay per click campaigns and other promotional efforts.

Affiliate Marketing Breakout

They understand the importance of keeping an eye on their stats. Knowing how many visitors your sites are getting, how many people are clicking on your affiliate links, and how many are buying is crucial to your success as an affiliate. It will alert you to strategies that aren't working so that you can replace them with strategies that do. Super affiliates check their stats often and use that information to fine-tune their efforts.

They are eager to learn. As the Internet evolves, so does affiliate marketing. New techniques and applications are coming out all the time, and if you ignore them, you could be left behind. Super affiliates understand that you can't learn it all in one sitting. Even if you were to learn everything there is to know about affiliate marketing today, there will be something new to learn tomorrow.

They don't mind taking risks. Just because the tried and true stuff is working, that doesn't mean that they won't attempt something new. It might work out and it might not, but super affiliates are willing to take a chance if there's the possibility of greater profits.

If you possess these traits, there's not much standing in the way of you making a nice passive income. If you don't, work on them. Without them, all the tips and techniques in the world won't be much help. The good news is that it's primarily a matter of attitude, and that's something you can always change if you want to badly enough.

Common Affiliate Mistakes

We all make mistakes. It's a fact of life. Even seasoned affiliate marketing pros are not immune to them. But there are certain mistakes that are common among those who are struggling to find their way as affiliates. Do any of these sound familiar to you?

Joining the wrong programs – Some affiliates make the mistake of joining affiliate programs just because of their high commission rates, or because someone else they know is doing well with them. But these things cannot necessarily be used to predict success in a particular situation.

Relying solely on graphic advertising – Banners and buttons are useful tools for affiliates, but they're not the be-all and end-all of affiliate marketing. They rarely generate nearly as many sales as a good product review or other useful content. There's nothing wrong with using graphics, just don't make that your only approach.

Promoting too many products – Some affiliates join so many programs that they can't keep up with them all. If keeping up with all of the products you're promoting is a full-time job, how will you have time to actually promote them?

Not promoting enough products – Other affiliates concentrate their efforts on just one or two products.

While it's good to have focus, expanding your offerings allows for greater income potential.

Failure to explore different methods of promotion – When you find something that brings in affiliate sales, it can be tempting to just stick with it and not try anything else. But there are many different ways to promote your affiliate links. If you don't give them a try, you could be missing out on a lot of profits.

Not reading the fine print – Every affiliate program has its own set of terms, and they vary greatly from program to program. If you don't read and heed them, you could miss out on commissions, or even be removed from the program for violations.

Spamming – With all of the spammers there are out there, you'd think there was a lot of money in it. But whether it's sending out unsolicited emails or creating slogs, spamming will get you nowhere fast. You'll lose the trust of your potential customers, and you could get in trouble with your ISP, your web host, and the search engines (and possibly even the law). If you're not familiar with the actions that could be considered spamming, take some time to learn about them before you go any further.

If you've made any of these mistakes, don't feel bad. Few marketers get through their entire affiliate career without a single blunder. Just correct what you can and keep moving forward.

Choosing Your Niche

If you want to make money online (and particularly with affiliate marketing), you need a niche. Or better yet, several niches. But each niche needs its own site and/or blog, its own mailing list, and its own affiliate programs for you to promote.

If you've been an affiliate for any length of time, you've almost certainly heard this advice. But it's amazing how many affiliates don't follow through with it. Or they try to follow through with it, but their "niche" is nothing more than a product category, and they don't tailor their marketing efforts to a specific market segment.

For the uninitiated, catering to specific niches might seem counterproductive. After all, by narrowing your focus, you're limiting yourself to prospects that fit into a certain small group with specific characteristics. Wouldn't it be better to offer a variety of products to a variety of people?

If you're Wal-Mart, that's not a bad approach to take. But for the rest of us, it's just too difficult to appeal to people with different interests, from different backgrounds, and with different needs. If you can focus on a small group, you can better meet their needs, and that's where your affiliate sales will come from.

Now that you know why working with niches is important, let's explore how to choose niches that are profitable. In order for a niche to make you money, it has to possess a few important characteristics:

It should ideally be something you're interested in. This is a topic you're going to be working with a lot for a while, and possibly for a long while depending on your marketing strategy. If a niche bores you to tears or otherwise doesn't appeal to you, you probably won't do very well with it.

It must have a sufficient audience. There must be a reasonable number of people who are interested enough in the topic to seek out information on it.

Without an audience, you'll have no one to sell to.

It should not be saturated. This simply means that there should not be a lot of other marketers catering to the same niche. The more marketers there are targeting the same group, the lower your chances of breaking in will be.

It should either be evergreen or an up and coming trend. Evergreen niches provide the best long-term income potential. Trends, which are on the rise, offer tremendous income potential in the beginning, but may or may not stand the test of time. It's fine to work with either type, but if you're following trends, be prepared to pursue the next big thing when you find that your current niche is on the decline.

The niche's target market should be willing and able to buy online. There are some niches that obviously wouldn't be a good choice for affiliate marketing, but for the most part, this is discovered by trial and error.

Once you've come up with a topic that interests you, you can start doing some research to determine whether or not it would make a good niche. A good tool for this purpose is the Google Adwords Keyword Tool (https://adwords.google.com/select/KeywordToolExtern al). Just type in your topic idea, and you'll be presented with a list of related keywords, along with a bar graph indicating the amount of competition for the keyword and its search volume. The best niches have low competition and high search volume.

When you find a niche that interests you and appears profitable, search for affiliate programs that would interest members of the target market. Put yourself in their shoes and think about the kinds of things you would be interested in buying. Then see what kinds of affiliate programs you can find that sell those things, and what percentage commissions they offer. If you like what you see, this could be a good niche for you.

There are no guarantees that any niche will be a winner. But if you do some research before jumping in, you can greatly increase your chances of success.

Choosing the Right Affiliate Programs

Many of the affiliate programs out there will accept just about any webmaster. Some are more selective, but they're usually just looking for affiliates who own sites with lots of traffic. Most do not take the subject matter of your site into consideration. So it's up to you to find programs that are a good fit.

One of the most important things to consider when choosing programs is whether they would appeal to your target market. Here's an extreme example: If you run a website about knitting, joining an affiliate program for a car parts company probably wouldn't be wise. Even becoming an affiliate for a company that sells supplies for other crafts might not make you much money. Stick close to the subject matter and become an affiliate for a yarn or pattern company.

If you plan to purchase pay per click ads to direct visitors straight to your affiliate link (or use other methods to do so), you'll have a lot more leeway as far as choosing programs. But it's still a good idea to stick with products you have at least some interest in. This will make it easier for you to write appealing ads, not to mention making your work more pleasant for you.

Commission isn't the most important thing when selecting affiliate programs, but it should certainly be considered. But it's best considered after you've found programs that are a good fit for your site and/or interests. Percentage is the first thing that most affiliates look at, but it's also crucial to consider the terms regarding payment of commissions. If there are conditions that could significantly reduce your commissions or make receiving payment difficult, you might want to reconsider.

Just like any other moneymaking opportunity, there is the potential for scams in affiliate marketing. So it's not a bad idea to do a little research before signing up with a company that you're not particularly familiar with. You could also go through an affiliate marketplace, which acts as an intermediary between companies and their affiliates. Some good ones to consider are Commission Junction, LinkShare and Pepperjam.

Should I Join Lots of Affiliate Programs or a Select Few?

A dilemma for many affiliate marketers is whether to go for quality or quantity in signing up for affiliate programs. On one hand, the more products you promote, the more potential income streams you have. On the other, signing up for just a few good programs allows you to concentrate more effort on promoting them.

For most affiliates, it's best to find a happy medium. Signing up for every program coming and going will just leave you terribly confused. But it is good to have several different things to promote. It keeps you from sounding like a broken record, trying to sell the same products over and over again (especially if you're promoting on a niche site or blog). And as long as you keep the numbers manageable, you'll be able to get to know your products well enough to recommend them with confidence.

Even if you're going the pay per click route, it's best not to sign up for too many programs. You'll have to spend some time writing ads and tracking your results for each one, and that's more time consuming than you might think. But you'll probably be able to handle more programs this way than you would if you were focusing exclusively on content-based promotion methods.

How to Get the Highest Possible Commission Rates

The commission rate determines how much money you make from each sale you generate. As stated before, it's not a good idea to select programs based solely on commission rate. But there's no denying that a high commission rate is more attractive than a low one.

The easiest way to get a high commission rate is to join an affiliate program that offers a high percentage to everyone who joins. But that's not the only way to do it.

Here are some tips for getting as much money as possible out of each sale.

Read the affiliate agreement carefully. You might just find an easy way to get bumped up to a higher commission rate, such as using a certain promotion method or selling a specific product. It's certainly worth looking into.

Make as many sales as possible. You'll make money from volume, and many merchants will also raise your commission rate if you reach a certain level of sales in a given amount of time. Some lay out the terms for such increases in their agreements, while others make adjustments on a case-bycase basis.

Recruit new affiliates. Some affiliate programs will pay you a commission for each sale your recruits make. And some will also raise commissions for your sales if you meet certain recruiting goals.

Pay attention to affiliate newsletters. They often announce affiliate contests in which the winners receive higher commissions or bonuses.

Email or call the affiliate manager and ask how you can get higher commissions. If you're generating a fair amount of sales, he might offer to raise your commission just to keep you happy. Or he might be able to tell you ways to get higher commissions that you weren't aware of. It never hurts to ask, as long as you do it nicely.

Do some comparison shopping. Look for programs similar to the ones you're promoting and see if they offer higher commissions. If they do, you could use this to help negotiate higher commissions with the merchant. And if he doesn't bite, you could consider switching to the other program. (Note: In order for this to work, you should already be generating a decent sales volume for the merchant you're negotiating with.)

Don't fall into the trap of thinking that commission rates are set in stone. Quite often, they are not. Most merchants recognize the benefits of keeping productive affiliates happy, so by working hard to generate sales, you increase your chances of getting a higher rate.

Pay per Lead Programs: Get Paid Without Making a Sale

Not every affiliate program requires you to generate sales for the merchant. Pay per lead programs, which pay out every time a referral signs up for something free, are growing in popularity. Companies are willing to pay for leads because it gives them the opportunity to make repeated contact with the potential customer.

Commissions in pay per lead programs are usually a set amount for each action. In most cases it's a rather small amount since the merchant is not making money directly from it. But if you find a good pay per lead program that converts well, you can get enough conversions to add up to a significant amount of money.

There are several varieties of pay per lead programs. Insurance companies often pay out for each referral that requests a quote. Some companies will pay you to recruit newsletter subscribers. Service providers often set up programs through which they pay affiliates to get people to sign up for free trials. You can also get paid for persuading people to request free stuff, such as product samples, eBooks, and software and information packets.

Pay per lead programs are great, but it's important to be selective with them. A company could feasibly pay affiliates to get them newsletter subscribers, then spam them or sell their addresses to spammers. Don't be lax on checking the background of the company just because you're not asking customers to buy anything. If something bad happens, it will damage their trust in you.

Running Pay per Click Ads: Get Paid for Sending Visitors to a Website

There is another type of affiliate program that allows you to make money without selling anything, and that's the pay per click program. Many affiliates purchase pay per click (PPC) ads to promote their own websites, and we'll cover that in more detail later.

Many beginning Internet marketers run pay per click ads such as Google Adsense on their websites. They reason that getting someone to click on a link is easier than getting someone to click on a link and buy something, and that's certainly true. The tradeoff is (in most cases) a lower payout for clicks than for actual sales. But if you can generate enough clicks, you can get a significant amount of passive income rolling in.

One thing that often trips affiliates up when it comes to running PPC ads is the assumption that they can just place the code on a page and forget about it. Then when they don't get the results that they've heard were possible, they figure it was all some sort of hoax and give up on it. But just like every other aspect of your website, pay per click ads often requires some tweaking and patience in order to get it right.

The first step to success with pay per click ads is making sure that the ones that appear on your site will appeal to your target market. In most cases, the ads are selected by an algorithm that examines your site's content and displays ads that relate well to it. If you find that you're frequently getting irrelevant ads, it's a good idea to examine your content and make sure that it's properly optimized for your targeted keywords. If you're just getting ads from certain advertisers that appear to not be going over well with your audience, you can usually block those ads.

Once you've got the right kinds of ads showing up, you need to test the ad blocks in various positions on the page. There's no one spot that's best for every website, so this is something that it pays to experiment with. Some sites find that ads in the sidebar do best, while others have better luck with them in the header or within the content of the page. You could also try out ad blocks of different sizes to see which ones generate the most clicks.

There are sites out there that generate huge amounts

of income using only Google Adsense and other types of PPC ads. But they are also good to use on sites where you promote pay per lead or pay per sale programs. As long as you take care to ensure that your site doesn't look like one big advertisement, pursuing multiple streams of income can work to your advantage.

Residual Income: Get Paid for the Same Sale Over and Over Again

With most affiliate programs, you promote a product, and if you make a sale, you get a commission on it. That's a good thing. But what if you could get paid over and over for the same sale? Wouldn't that be even better?

This is why many affiliates focus their efforts on programs that offer residual income. When they promote things like web hosting, membership sites and the like, they get a commission each month for as long as the customer keeps the service or remains a member. After they've made a few sales, it adds up to a nice monthly income.

Of course, not everyone will be a lifelong customer. But if you're promoting good products and services to the right people, a great many of them will stick with those products and services for months or years. In a year's time, you'll make twelve times more money from the sale as you would have with a one-off sale.

There's some sort of membership or ongoing service that will appeal to just about any niche. And if you can't find one for yours, consumables are the next best thing. Vitamins, pet food and other things that we have to buy again when we run out of them offer the potential for regular income if the customers are loyal. But it's important to seek out high quality products if you plan to go this route. Otherwise, you'll probably end up making one-time sales anyway.

Adding some programs that offer residual income into your affiliate marketing mix will allow you to earn more money with the same amount of effort. If you need ideas, most affiliate networks offer a search function that will help you find the right products to promote. If not, drop them an email. They are usually happy to help, because their affiliates' success is their success, too.

Domains and Affiliate Marketing

Most affiliate marketers are no stranger to the domain name market. At the very least, they probably have a domain name for their website or blog. And some have dozens of domains in their possession.

There are a few ways that domains can be used in

affiliate marketing. Many affiliates create niche sites or blogs for the sole purpose of promoting affiliate programs. Some also purchase domains to redirect to their affiliate links. This makes the URL shorter, easier to remember and more appealing.

If you're serious about affiliate marketing, you'll probably end up with several domains. But it is possible to go overboard with them. Some affiliates feel the need to buy a domain for every affiliate program they join. Not only is that expensive, it can also get extremely confusing.

Even if you are buying domains to redirect to your affiliate links, you don't necessarily have to buy one for each and every program. If you belong to several programs in the same niche, you could use a general domain name and create sub domains for each program. For example, if your niche is herb gardening, you might be an affiliate for a seed company and the author of a book on herb gardening. But instead of buying a domain for each program, you could get a domain like herbgardening.com and create the sub domains seeds.herbgardening.com and book.herbgardening.com to redirect to your affiliate links.

It's also possible to be too conservative when it comes to buying domains. In general, it's best to have a domain for each niche you're in. And in some cases, you might find that you need two or three for the same niche. There are no hard and fast rules. Just do what's most comfortable (or most profitable) for you.

Choosing Domains

Back in the early days of the World Wide Web, it wasn't too difficult to get any domain name you wanted.

Today, it's a different story. It's pretty much impossible to get a good one-word .com domain name, and it's becoming increasingly difficult to get good names with other extensions.

But if you're choosing targeted niches, one-word domain names probably aren't your best bet anyway. They don't have much SEO value, because Internet users don't often do searches for just one word. They are more likely to search for phrases, so domain names that contain those phrases are better choices. If you can snag a domain name that contains your targeted keywords, you'll have an easier time getting good search engine rankings.

A domain name shouldn't be too long, though. If it is, it will be hard to remember. It's true that most visitors will click on a link from another site or bookmark your site if they're interested, but if someone hears your domain name and wants to visit, wouldn't you want him to be able to do so? If he can't remember it, you miss out on a potential sale. For the same reason, it's wise to avoid using abbreviations, numbers in place of words ("4u" instead of "for you," etc.), and words that are difficult to spell.

There is some debate as to whether you should use hyphens in domain names. At one time, it appeared that search engines favored domains with hyphens between the words when ranking for the keyword phrase appearing in the domain name. But today, it doesn't really appear to make a difference. Now the most common reason for using hyphenated domains is to get a name that is already taken in the non-hyphenated form. As long as you don't use more than one or two hyphens, it shouldn't have too much of an impact on your type-in traffic.

As far as extensions go, it's a good idea to try for a .com domain first. Even today, it's the most familiar extension to the average Internet user. But if you absolutely can't get a good .com for your niche, try another extension. .net is a good one, and .org gives the impression that your site is trustworthy (even though anyone can get an .org domain). If you're promoting products that are seen on TV, a .tv extension is perfectly acceptable.

If you get a really good domain, it might be to your advantage to get several forms of it. Hyphenated, non-hyphenated, .com, and .net are good variations to have. You might even consider purchasing common misspellings of your domain. There's no need to do this for every domain, but if you're lucky enough to get your hands on one that contains a frequently searched keyword phrase, it could be worth the cost.

A good domain name can certainly have a positive impact on your traffic. The pool of available domains is constantly shrinking, but with a little creativity you can come up with something that's both memorable and appealing to the search engines.

A Word about SEO

Search engine optimization (SEO) is one of the most cost-effective ways to get traffic to any website. It's one of the first things that most affiliates learn, so we won't go into it in depth here. But it's such an important subject that it deserves to be revisited from time to time.

SEO is an ongoing process. It's not one of those "set it and forget it" things. Once you've done your initial optimization it becomes easier to maintain it, but you must keep working at it. Search engines change their algorithms frequently, so it's crucial to continually check on your rankings. That way, if they drop, you can take action before you lose too much traffic.

If your site ranks highly in the search engines, you won't need to spend a lot of money on pay per click and other forms of advertising. You can concentrate your efforts on building incoming links and creating new content to keep your visitors happy.

Pay Per Click Strategies

Performing search engine optimization is one of the least expensive and most effective ways to get traffic to your site. But it's not the only way to get visitors from search engines. Pay per click advertising (PPC) requires an investment, but it can greatly boost your affiliate traffic and sales if used correctly.

We've all seen the "Sponsored Links" at the top and

sides of search result pages. Those are actually PPC ads. (They're also found on some websites.) Some Internet users have grown rather blind to these, but there are still plenty who click on them. Besides, when you run a PPC campaign, you're not paying for each time your ad is shown. You're paying for each time someone clicks on it.

Affiliates use PPC ads for a few different purposes. One is to get visitors to a website or blog where they promote affiliate products. Another is to send them to a squeeze page, where they can sign up for a newsletter or e-course. And sometimes they just direct visitors straight to an affiliate link. Your approach will vary depending on which of these is your objective.

If you're directing PPC ads to an affiliate link, it's important to use keywords that attract people who are interested in buying. Otherwise, you're pretty much wasting your money. For instance, if you're an affiliate for a company that sells leather gloves, try to think like someone who is interested in buying a pair. Perhaps he has a brand or color in mind. You could try using something like "black leather gloves" or "Cole Haan leather gloves" as your keywords. Or if you're targeting bargain shoppers, "discount leather gloves" might be a good keyword phrase.

If you're trying to get opt-in subscribers, you would use a much different strategy. The idea here is to lure prospects with the promise of information. That way you won't be paying for visitors who are interested in buying something right now and will click away when they see a squeeze page. Keyword phrases that contain words such as "learn" or "information" are well suited to this purpose. The ad text should further emphasize the promise of information.

Those who want site visitors might use a similar approach as far as keywords go. In order to get visitors who are actually looking for what you have to offer, be as specific as possible. If you feature reviews on your site, be sure to include the word "reviews" in your keyword phrases. If it's a blog, use the word "blog," and so on. The ad text should be compelling, but usually not pushy.

Writing effective PPC ads almost always requires trial and error. You'll need to implement a tracking method in order to see whether or not your ads work. If you're directing traffic to your own site (or using redirects for your affiliate links), the statistical software will tell you what you need to know. Most affiliate programs also offer stats tracking that will tell you how many visitors made it to your affiliate link and how many made purchases.

If you find that you're getting lots of traffic but few sales or click-throughs to your affiliate link, it's time to go back to the drawing board. Very low traffic can be a sign of a poorly written ad. But if you're getting a high percentage of conversions out of that small amount of traffic, it probably just means that you've done a good job of choosing highly targeted keywords.

Choosing Pay per Click Networks

Ask any Internet marketer to name a PPC network, and there's a good chance that you'll hear the name Google Adwords. It stands to reason that since Google is the number one search engine, its pay per click offering is one of the most popular. Many affiliates make their first foray into PPC with Adwords, and they often stick with it.

Adwords has the potential to bring you lots of traffic.

But it's not the only PPC network that's worth using. There are many others to consider, including:

Microsoft Adcenter – Displays ads on the Bing search engine and the Microsoft content network.

Yahoo Search Marketing – Displays ads on the Yahoo search engine.

7Search – Supplies search results and ads to over 500 search engines, blogs and websites.

Adbrite – Supplies ads through a content network.

Bidvertiser – Supplies ads through a content network.

After Google, Microsoft and Yahoo are the next biggest players in the pay per click game. But that doesn't mean that all other networks are a waste of time. Smaller PPC networks have an advantage when it comes to pricing. On average, advertisers pay less per click than they would on the "Big Three." So if you're on a tight budget, you may do better to give them a try.

Each PPC network has rules that advertisers must follow, and it's imperative that you read over them carefully. Some do not allow advertisers to use direct affiliate links. Some have minimum deposits that you must make. And all have certain guidelines for the ads themselves. You can save yourself a lot of headaches by making sure that you understand the terms fully before placing your first ad.

Content Sites and Affiliate Marketing

Early on, content sites made up a large portion of the World Wide Web. There's a lot more out there now, but good content sites still have a great deal of value. They serve as sources of information, and information is still something that most Internet users look for on a regular basis.

One of the advantages of content sites is that they are easy to maintain. It takes some work to get them set up, but once you've got everything in place, you don't have to keep it updated on a regular schedule. Adding some new content from time to time is a good idea, but it's not absolutely necessary. If you pay special attention to SEO when building a content site, you won't even have to put a lot of effort in to promoting it.

Another good thing about content sites is that it's easier for visitors to find the information they need than it is on a blog. A content site's navigation is usually organized by topic, allowing users to find what they're looking for with just a couple of clicks. Blogs, on the other hand, are organized chronologically. You can use categories to make posts somewhat easier to find, but older posts are still left in the shadows of new ones.

Content sites do not have to have pages upon pages of information to be useful. In fact, if you're working with a sufficiently narrow niche, a mini site with just a few pages will do. Instead of trying to provide huge amounts of information, concentrate on creating a few pieces of great content.

The keys to getting traffic to a content site are providing informative content and optimizing it for keywords that your target market would use. Get some backlinks coming in and do a little initial promotion, and you can often leave the site alone and let it work its magic for a while. But don't forget to check your stats periodically, so that if you lose ground in the search engines or conversions drop you can find and fix the problem.

Getting Fellow Webmasters to Help Promote Your Site

Promoting a website can be a lot of work. But you don't

have to do it all yourself. In fact, it's best if you don't. Enlisting the help other webmasters will allow you to gain exposure on their websites, and that can seriously boost your search rankings. The days of the link exchange have passed, but there are other ways to get assistance from fellow site owners.

One way you can get your links on other websites is by submitting articles to article directories. Article directories are designed to provide free content for webmasters, and anyone can submit articles. You're allowed to add links and a resource box to your articles, and anyone who uses them must leave these things intact. If you write good articles that are related to your niche, fellow webmasters will place them on their sites and you'll get back links and traffic from it.

You could also contact bloggers in your niche and ask if they would allow you to write a guest post for them. In exchange for the free exclusive content, you can request that they link to your site. If it's a popular blog, you could get lots of traffic for a long time to come.

And then there are joint ventures. You could contact other site owners and see if they would be interested in sponsoring a contest, producing an information product or participating in some other type of marketing activity with you. Both of you would work on it, both of your names and URLs would be on it, and both would promote it. And each of you would gain new traffic and back links.

By creating quality content, you can gain back links from webmasters who find it useful. But it certainly doesn't hurt to be a little more proactive about it. These methods won't cost you a dime, and they have the potential to bring you lots of traffic and better search engine rankings.

Blogs and Affiliate Marketing

Blogs are well suited to affiliate marketing. Internet users enjoy reading them because they are interactive and personal. This makes them excellent relationship builders for affiliates. And readers know that they are usually updated regularly, so when they find one they like they keep coming back. This gives you infinite opportunities to make a sale.

Some affiliates get their start in affiliate marketing by mentioning products in posts on an existing blog. For niche blogs, this works very well. But with few exceptions, blogs with general topics tend to generate fewer affiliate sales. If you're looking to earn commissions by blogging, you're better off to start a blog with a narrow focus. Or better yet, several of them.

For affiliate marketers, part of the beauty of blogging is

that blogs are so easy to set up and run. Many web hosts provide automated installation of blogging platforms such as WordPress in their hosting packages. You can write posts and pages without having to know HTML, and it's very easy to make modifications to a blog's appearance and functionality.

Perhaps the hardest thing about blogging is coming up with good niche topics. For best results, you need a topic that's pretty narrow, but that generates a lot of interest. It should also be something that you are interested in, because you're the one who will be writing content about it on an ongoing basis. If you have no interest in or knowledge about the subject, it will be difficult to do that.

Another thing to consider when choosing a niche is how much competition there is in it. The less competition there is, the better. You can get a general idea of the amount of competition in a given niche by plugging related keywords into the Google Adwords Keyword Suggestion Tool (https://adwords.google.com/select/KeywordToolExternal). The tool will also tell you how much search volume keywords receive, giving you an idea of the amount of interest.

If you choose a good niche and join affiliate programs that will interest your audience, you can do very well with affiliate marketing through a blog. With some promotion and regular updating, a blog can be a very effective commission generator.

Promoting Affiliate Products on a Blog

It can be tempting to just throw some graphical ads in the header and sidebar of your blog in an effort to make sales. These types of ads can be effective, but they're rarely as effective as mentions of the products in your blog posts. If you are building a rapport with your readers, they will be interested in the products you recommend, or even just mention.

Just casually working in a reference to a product is the simplest way to get your affiliate link out there. You could mention using the product, or discuss a news story that involves it. If the product appeals to your target market, you should get some clicks, and eventually some conversions.

But the most effective way to generate affiliate sales is to review the products you're promoting. If the product is appropriate for your audience, they will appreciate an in-depth review. And if you've established trust with your readers, a recommendation could be extremely lucrative.

Reviews are also great for bringing in search engine visitors who are interested in making a purchase. Those who are debating whether or not to buy a specific product often do searches for reviews of it. If the search brings them to your blog post, and they like what they see, there's a good chance that they will click your affiliate link and complete the transaction. There's also a good chance that they will bookmark your blog.

When doing product reviews, it is essential to be honest. Your first instinct might be to avoid saying anything bad about something that could make you money, but if every product gets glowing reviews, your readers are going to get suspicious. It's better to lose a sale and keep your readers' trust than vice versa. If you lose a reader's trust, you may never get another opportunity to make a sale to him.

Blogs and affiliate marketing are a match made in

heaven. But in order to get the most out of your blog, you must keep it updated with fresh, high quality content. If you can't work an affiliate link into every post, that's okay. In fact, throwing in a promotion-free post every now and then will keep your audience from feeling like they're nothing more than a prospect to you.

Podcasting

The days of the Internet being a text-only medium are long since over. Today it's filled with all sorts of sights and sounds. There are elaborate flash applications, games, videos, radio stations and much, much more.

Audio on the Web is a wonderful thing for a lot of reasons. It makes it more accessible for the visually impaired, and it makes it easier for those who learn better by hearing than by reading to grasp what's being said. It also makes the Internet more personal. Even the best writer can't fully convey the emotion of what someone is saying in print.

In light of these factors, it's no wonder that affiliates have taken to podcasting as a means of promoting their websites and products. This gives them a different avenue for building relationships and loyalty with their target market. It also makes their messages more portable if they make their podcasts available for download, because listeners can put it on their MP3 players and take it with them wherever they go.

A podcast is more or less the audio equivalent of a blog. You can use it to inform your audience, or to provide commentary on various topics. It's also a great medium for doing interviews with professionals in your niche, or even merchants whose products you are promoting.

To get started in podcasting, there are a few things you'll need. The first is a good microphone. This is important because it will reduce the amount of background noise and accurately capture your voice. A good sound card is also something you should have in your computer. Additionally, you will need software such as Audacity to capture your podcast, add in music and other sounds, and compress the files. Some podcasters also utilize a mixer, but that's not a necessity when you're starting out. You can always buy one later on if you feel the need.

You have a few options for posting your podcast. One is to post it on iTunes. To do this, you'll need to upload it to a server and submit your RSS feed to iTunes. Making your podcast available via iTunes lends an air of legitimacy, but listeners will have to have an iTunes account and software in order to access it.

Another way to make your podcast available is to post through a blog. There is some wonderful WordPress plug-ins (such as PodPress) that makes posting podcasts very easy. And if you include a link to your RSS feed on your blog, listeners can subscribe so that they may listen to new content as soon as it becomes available. You can also include some descriptive text and clickable affiliate links on the podcast page if you're publishing through your own blog.

Podcasts can be short tidbits of information, or they can be more like radio shows and run for a half hour or more. If you're working with a small niche, a few minutes worth of content should be sufficient. It will also be more easily digestible than a long podcast.

Not every affiliate uses podcasts, and they're not one of those things that you have to do in order to succeed. But they can add greatly to your marketing efforts. If you can come up with topics for a blog, you can come up with topics for a podcast, and you don't need lots of expensive equipment to get started. So it can't hurt to at least give it a try.

Marketing with Videos

Anyone who has been living under a rock for the past few years might not have heard of YouTube. But the rest of us know that it's one of the hottest sites on the Internet. Anyone can submit videos, and visitors that enjoy a video are often eager to spread the word about it.

Affiliate marketers are often intimidated by the idea of creating YouTube videos. Some of them are very polished, and you can tell that no expense has been spared in making them. But videos do not have to be professionally made in order to be effective. Even funny home videos have been successfully used to get traffic!

Even if you're on a tight budget, you can create videos for YouTube. Windows users have a handy program called Windows Movie Maker on their computers, and they can use it to make videos without even needing a video camera. You can use images and text to get your point across, and add some music or a voice recording for sound. If you have a digital camcorder or webcam, you can use video and audio from that as well.

Another popular tool for marketers is a piece of software called Camtasia. Camtasia allows you to capture video from your computer screen and audio from a microphone to create videos. This works very nicely for marketers in technology and Internet marketing niches. With it, you can make great instructional videos with ease.

You can mention your website and affiliate links in YouTube videos. It's also a good idea to include the links you're promoting in the video's description. And after you've uploaded a video to the site, you can add annotations to it that include links. This ensures that even if users embed the video onto their own site, viewers can easily click through if they are interested.

YouTube videos are viral marketing at its best. A good video could potentially get thousands of views and bring lots of traffic to your website or affiliate link. And as easy as it is to create videos, anyone can take advantage of this powerful marketing channel.

Email Marketing

Aside from talking in person, email is the least expensive way we can communicate with others. It's not surprising that marketers realized the benefits of email early on. Unfortunately, scammers and spammers also seized the opportunity to make contact with people at very little cost, and they haven't let up since.

The prevalence of spam, along with Internet users' dedication to avoiding it, has prompted some critics to conclude that email marketing is dead. But tell that to affiliates with large lists and equally large incomes, and they will laugh. They'll tell you that as long as you play by the rules, email provides an unparalleled opportunity to stay in contact with your target market.

What are these rules? Here's a summary.

Gain your audience's trust. These days, people do not take giving up their email address lightly. Those, who have read your website or blog and found it useful and forthright, are most likely to sign up for your mailing list. Some of your subscribers will be people who just happened by your opt-in page, but the majority are usually people who are already familiar with what you do and know you're on the up-and-up.

Don't waste your subscribers' time. Instead of just sending out emails to keep your name out there, provide them with something of value. It could be helpful tips, product recommendations or links to relevant news items. Whatever it is, put yourself in the reader's shoes. If you wouldn't be interested, neither would they. And disinterested subscribers quickly become former subscribers.

Keep it fairly short. Marketers often feel obligated to send out a long email with several articles. But few people are willing to wade through a long email any more, even if it's on a subject they're passionate about. A short note or a single article is much better received. If you have more than that to say to your readers, direct them to your website.

Avoid making every email a hard sell. Your objective is to make money, but if you pursue it too aggressively, you'll turn your readers off. There's nothing wrong with openly promoting products, just don't do it every time you hit the "Send" button.

Take steps to avoid spam filters. Try to make sure that email subjects and content do not appear spammy, and remind subscribers to whitelist your email address.

Honor all unsubscribed requests. Sending out unwanted emails isn't going to change anyone's mind. If anything, it will make them more determined not to listen to anything you have to say. And it will also give you a bad reputation, making others who hear reports of unsolicited email wary of signing up for your list.

List Building

It's a myth that marketers must have tons of subscribers in order for a mailing list to be worthwhile. Lists with thousands and thousands of addresses on them might sound impressive, but they're often less effective than smaller lists. That's because such large lists are rarely well targeted.

When building a list, it's important to keep your target market in mind. It's easy to fall into the trap of trying to appeal to a broad audience in order to get more subscribers, but that won't help you make sales. If the products you're promoting only appeal to a small market segment, having a lot of subscribers who don't fit into that segment does you no good whatsoever.

Obviously, you need to get targeted traffic to your opt-in page if you want to build a targeted mailing list. That can be accomplished with good SEO, pay per click ads and other promotional efforts. But it's also important to create a squeeze page that will persuade only the people who fit into your target market to sign up.

One way to accomplish this is to give away a digital product that will appeal to your niche to new subscribers. Free gifts will not only help you get subscribers, they will help ensure that those subscribers are interested in what you're offering. If you were giving away a physical product you might get some takers that only wanted the freebie to give to someone else, but not many Internet users will sign up for a mailing list to get an eBook or audio that is of no interest to them. And if they're not interested in the freebie, they're probably not interested in your niche.

When it comes to mailing list subscribers, quality is far more important than quantity. So don't spread yourself too thin and try to attract too broad of an audience. Stick close to your niche, and you'll get the right kinds of subscribers.

Selling to Your List

Once you've started your mailing list, it's time to think about what you're going to do with it. Sure, you're going to attempt to make sales, but how will you go about it? Will you discuss the products that you're promoting in your emails? Will you alert readers to site updates in an effort to get more repeat visits to your website? Or will you send informative articles and advice as a way to build trust with subscribers?

Affiliates frequently include references to products in their emails, along with an affiliate link. This gives the reader the opportunity to buy without having to go through your website. This could work for readers that are already considering the product, but for everyone else it's important to make it easy to visit your website for more information. Link to a full product review if you've done one, or include a link to your site in your signature.

Some marketers update their sites frequently instead of sending a lot of content out to their mailing lists. They might add a new article or review every other week, and then send out an email announcing it to subscribers. This avoids wasting their time if they are not interested in the content, and gets them to pay a visit to your website if they are.

Even if you're not trying to sell directly with your emails, you could include a link to a popular product in your signature line, along with a few words about it. Write the blurb with the same care you'd use when writing a pay per click ad, and try to pique the reader's curiosity. This is a good way to make sales without being too pushy.

Affiliate Marketing and the Social Web: A Brief Overview

Over the past several years, the Internet has become more and more social. This has made it more appealing for your average Web surfer. And for affiliate marketers, it has opened up many more avenues to reach potential customers.

Here are some of the social applications that affiliates can use to build back links, get site visitors and build relationships:

Forums – The forum is one of the oldest types of interactive application online. Forums make it possible for groups to have discussions on any topic. Part of their appeal is the ability for users to check the boards at their leisure without having to be in front of the computer at the same time as everyone else.

Micro-blogging services – Twitter is the most popular micro-blogging application. It's a simple concept: users post short messages (140 characters or less) for other users to read. Users can follow the "tweets" of people they know or find interesting.

Social networks – MySpace and Facebook are two of the most popular social networking websites. They allow users to create profile pages, interact with other users and add them as friends. Features vary from network to network, but you may be able to post photos, video and audio, send messages to other users, join groups and more.

Social news, media and bookmarking sites – These sites attempt to highlight the most popular news stories, web pages and multimedia on the Web. They are great sources of traffic if used correctly.

Joining forums and social networking groups that are relevant to your niche is an effective way to connect with your target market. But it's important not to just jump in and start overtly promoting your affiliate links. Not only will this annoy the group's members, it could get you labeled as a spammer and kicked out. Instead, join in the conversations and be friendly and helpful. Include a site or affiliate link in your signature or on your profile page, and let members make the decision to click on it without undue influence.

Twitter doesn't allow much space to get your point across, so you'll have to be a little more creative. If you put an affiliate link in every tweet, you'll end up with no followers. If you never promote anything, you'll end up with no sales. The same advice about being friendly and helpful in social networks applies here, but posting an affiliate link here and there won't get you in trouble.

Submitting links to social news and media sites is a favorite traffic generating method of many affiliate marketers. But in order for it to work, you must submit links that follow the rules of the site and will appeal to users. The users are the ones who will vote it up or down, and if you submit links that they find useless, boring or spammy, you're just wasting your time.

If you use any of these applications for non-business purposes, it's usually best to start a new account for your affiliate endeavors, as long as the site or network allows it. That way you won't have to worry about coming across as unprofessional. But that doesn't mean you shouldn't be yourself when you're representing your affiliate business in social applications. It just means that you should always be the most professional version of yourself.

As an affiliate marketer, you can't afford to overlook the

social Web as a means of generating sales. Blogging is a

good start, but if you're not exploring other

applications, you're missing out on some very effective

relationship builders.

Using Affiliate Data Feeds

Many career affiliates use data feeds to add product

pages or links to their sites. Data feeds are database

files that contain information about all of a merchant's

products, usually including the product name,

description, image, price and your affiliate link. Some

data feeds also contain other information.

Some merchants make their data feeds available to

every affiliate. Others charge a fee for providing them.

And some only provide data feeds to their top

performing affiliates. Affiliate networks sometimes

make all of their feeds available to approved affiliates

for a one-time fee.

In order to use a data feed, you'll need a program that can export databases into HTML. Alternatively, you could get a programmer to translate the files into web pages. Either way, data feeds enable you to add any number of products to your website quickly and easily. And by using the latest data feed from a merchant, you can ensure that you list all products that are currently available and none that are not.

There are a couple of different ways in which you can use data feeds. One is to create an online store-type site. You can separate products into categories, and display links to descriptions of individual products on the category pages. You can also add specific types of products to pages with content related to those products. For example, if you have an article about running shoes on your site and you are an affiliate for a shoe company, you could display links to various styles of running shoes on that page.

Data feeds make it easy to set up an affiliate store, or to add links to an existing affiliate site. You can even set it up so that your site is updated automatically if the merchant makes its feeds available on a server. Just remember that the best performing sites include more than just a bunch of affiliate links. Adding some original content will make your site more attractive to the search engines and to visitors.

Using Calls to Action

We've covered some of the most popular and effective ways to promote your affiliate links. But whether you use one, a few, or all of these, there is a simple thing that can have a major impact on your success. And that's the call to action.

Just like it sounds, a call to action is a statement that encourages the reader, listener or viewer to take action. This action could be making a purchase, signing up for a newsletter, or visiting your website. But no matter what action is desired, it is imperative that you make it clear to the reader what you want him to do.

All too often, affiliates avoid making calls to action. This may be true for several reasons:

1. They worry about being too pushy. They fear that customers won't like being told what to do, and if they try they will head for the hills.

2. They feel that making a direct call to action will insult the prospect's intelligence. After all, when people read a sales page or pitch, they know that you want them to buy something, right?

3. They think calls to action are unnecessary. They

reason that if the prospect wants to buy, he will do what it takes to make the purchase without any encouragement.

4. They're not sure how to make a call to action. Should they say "Buy this now!" or be more subtle about it?

But if you fail to make that call to action, there's a good chance that you'll also fail to make a sale. In this day and age, people are bombarded with so much information that they don't have the capacity to process it all. So if you don't make it crystal clear that you're asking them to make a purchase, it's quite possible that they won't. Even if they are interested in the product you're promoting, they might just think, "Well that's interesting," and get on with their lives.

How you make your call to action will depend somewhat on where you're using it. Here are a few guidelines for some of the promotional tools you've learned about.

Blogs – Blogs are more about building relationships than selling. Calls to action are still important here, but they should be a bit more subtle than they would in a sales letter. Instead of asking readers to buy something now, mention products and include a link. Advise them to "Click here for more information" or something to that effect.

Content sites – Since content sites are less personal than blogs, there's no harm in cutting straight to the chase when asking for the sale. If you've provided solid, relevant information to the reader, a powerful call to action will entice him to check out what you're offering, not turn him off.

Videos and podcasts – If you're doing a video blog or

podcast, it's usually best to stick with the same type of approach you would use with a text blog and not be too pushy. But if you're creating videos that are clearly promotional, there's nothing wrong with squarely asking for the sale or optin.

Email – In email newsletters or announcements, it pays to be rather obvious about your intentions. It's just too easy for the reader to close the email and forget about it, or worse yet delete it. Making it a point to directly tell the reader to buy the product or visit your website to learn more will pay off.

Social networks – With few exceptions, blatant promotion is not allowed in social networks. But you can include a call to action in forum signatures and on profile pages. One technique that's generally well received is using a teaser to entice readers to click the link and learn more.

Twitter – Calls to action on Twitter may be subtle or overt. But unless your Twitter account is geared toward motivated buyers or deal seekers, it's not usually a good idea to include a directive to buy something very often.

Don't be intimidated by calls to action. They've been used in sales letters and other promotional materials since their inception, so there aren't many people who will find them offensive. And if someone already has some degree of interest in what you're offering, a little nudge certainly won't change their mind. It will just push them in the right direction.

In Affiliate Marketing, You Get What You Put In

Since the Internet became available to the average person, there have been lots of people looking for ways to make easy money online. And there probably always will be. But in life, there is no free lunch. This is just as true on the Internet as it is in the "real" world.

Affiliate marketing does present the opportunity to make lots of money. And once you get started with it, you can maintain that income without a huge amount of effort. But finding a niche, selecting affiliate programs and doing what it takes to effectively promote the products takes some time and effort. When those who are looking for a free ride discover this, they are ready to throw in the towel.

But if you're serious about making money as an affiliate, you can generate great wealth. Those gurus that are making so much really aren't much different from the average Internet user. They just had the determination they needed to seek out great affiliate opportunities and work on their promotional efforts until they got it right. We can learn a lot from their experience, but we still have to do our part to find what it takes to make it in a given niche.

You don't necessarily have to make affiliate marketing a full-time pursuit in order to make big money. But you must have patience, and you must be willing to work at it. If you can use a computer, you can make a good living with affiliate marketing. Do not let getting off to a slow start deter you. Let it be your motivation for finding the best programs and promotional methods!